Shapes

Written by Margie Burton, Cathy French

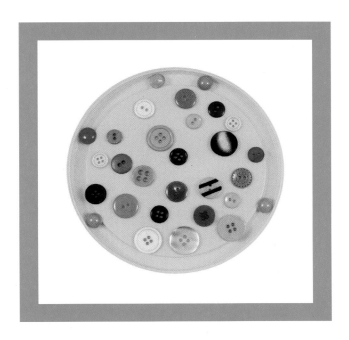

The clock is a circle.

The pie is a circle.

The rug is a square.

The book is a square.

The cake is a rectangle.

The flag is a rectangle.

The tree is a triangle.

The kite is a triangle.

Ordinal Numbers

by Kristin Sterling

Lerner Publications · Minneapolis

Ordinal numbers tell us the order of things.

1st 2nd 3rd 4th

The little boy is **first** in line.

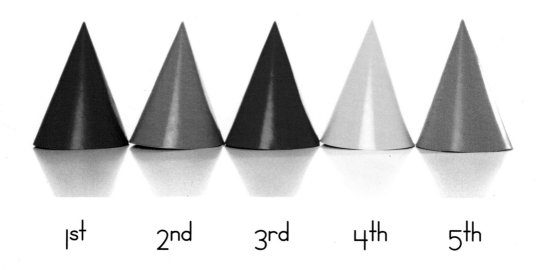

1st   2nd   3rd   4th   5th

The red hat is **second** in line.

1st   2nd   3rd   4th

The sad dog is **third** in line.

The oldest child is **fourth** in line.

1st   2nd   3rd   4th   5th

The smallest doll is **fifth** in line.

Which animal is third in line?